MADELINE ISLAND
and the Chequamegon Region

MADELINE ISLAND &

THE

Chequamegon Region

•

JOHN O. HOLZHUETER

•

THE STATE HISTORICAL SOCIETY OF WISCONSIN

1986

Library of Congress Cataloging in Publication Data:
Holzhueter, John O. 1935-
  Madeline Island & the Chequamegon region
  1. Chequamegon region, Wis.—History.
2. Madeline Island, Wis.—History I. Title.
F587.A8H64   917.75'21   74-20919
ISBN 0-87020-146-8

                        THIRD PRINTING: 1986

FIFTEEN years have passed since the State Historical Society commissioned this booklet. It happened that at the same time Alice E. Smith was completing her monumental first volume in *The History of Wisconsin* series, drawing together the accumulation of her forty-five years of distinguished scholarship about Wisconsin and the Upper Great Lakes region, and I was fortuitously assigned a temporary office directly next to hers. She graciously shared both her notes and her chapter drafts, and when it came time in the summer of 1972 to forsake the library for a field trip to the island, Alice asked if she could join me and George Roeder (then a *History of Wisconsin* researcher) who had agreed to help drive. We leapt at the opportunity: who could teach us more? For Alice, however, it was a sentimental request: she wanted to traverse the state, north to south, one last time before retiring to California.

The journey was magical for all three of us. We scarcely touched a main highway as we sought out landmarks whose significance embraced countless interlocking historical trends spanning more than three centuries. One thing Alice insisted upon: surveying the southern tip of Madeline Island on foot, walking the same ground she knew Pierre Le Sueur had walked in 1693 and looking out over the same unchanging but perpetually renewed waters of Chequamegon Bay as he had. Although others certainly had visited the island before Le Sueur, no one knows exactly where they built their shelters and made their camps. With Le Sueur, the tie to the past and to the early French explorers and traders is secure, tangible.

With Alice's accumulated knowledge at my beck and call, it seemed impossible then that new dimensions soon would be added to what I had learned about the place. But no sooner had she retired in 1973 and I had joined the Society's staff later that same year than a flood of new studies began to come to hand. They are important because they shifted our focus from the French explorer to the Indian residents. They shattered our assumptions about the all-powerful European being able to come and go as he pleased, at the mercy only of the twists and turns of Europe's economy and monarchies.

From Bruce Trigger we have learned that Indians, not the "explorers," decided who could explore what and when; that Indians, not the French, were in charge at least until the 1800's; and that Indians regarded the light-skinned newcomers, despite their weaponry and tools and ornaments, as definitely inferior. From Marcel Trudel we have learned the true enormity of the white community's minority status. From Selwyn Dewdney and Calvin Martin we have learned that Madeline Island possesses a religious importance among the Chippewa akin to that of Rome or Jerusalem to Catholics and Jews. From W. J. Eccles we have learned that diplomacy, not the fur trade, was probably the principal reason that Europeans and later Americans exerted the horrendous efforts required to maintain western outposts, hoping eventually to gain the rights from the various tribes to enormous chunks of the continent, beating their colonizing competitors while ingratiating themselves with the Indians and helping the tribes to keep peace among themselves.

This summary only skims the surface, of course, and many more new findings and interpretations will come as we unravel the intricacies of Native American communities and ethics. One has only to read Nancy Lurie's splendid account of Wisconsin's Indian developments during the last quarter century to realize that the tale is still unfolding. Both Pierre Le Sueur and Alice Smith understood that full well as they gazed across Chequamegon Bay.

Neither Alice, George, nor I has made that north-south trek since, and it is my misfortune not to have seen Alice again. Our journey, however, remains a fresh memory, for on it I developed not only a fondness for one of Wisconsin's most beautiful spots, but also a firmer appreciation for how knowledge of the past truly does enrich the present. In a way I am glad that the three of us cannot make the trip again. It would never be the same. No moment in history ever is, and, in its own small way through this booklet, that trip, too, has become a part of the past of Madeline Island and the Chequamegon region.

J. O. H.

January, 1986

ILLUSTRATIONS

A selection of photographs of Madeline Island and environs, selected from the Iconographic Collections of the State Historical Society of Wisconsin, follows page 32. The Society gratefully acknowledges the contributions of E. Leland Cooper, Leo Capser, Hamilton Nelson Ross, and Elizabeth Abernathy Hull, whose photographic collections found their way into our pictorial archives in Madison.

WHEN the United States Senate in June, 1969, approved creation of the Apostle Islands National Lakeshore Area, it acknowledged what visitors to the region have known for more than 300 years. It was, to quote the first visitor of record who arrived in 1659, "beautiful." A nineteenth-century guest responded more romantically. "It looks," he wrote, "like a fairy scene, and everything about it is enchantment." Somehow, through a combination of luck, remoteness, failure of entrepreneurs to develop any significant industry, and owners who appreciated it, this "fairy scene" remains beautiful, and it has sufficiently enchanted both Congress and the legislature of Wisconsin so that much of it now is in public hands.

While verdant promise and glittering waters surpass the region's other charms, the history of the Apostle Islands easily outdistances the histories of most U.S. wilderness areas in flavor and interest. Father Marquette and John Jacob Astor are associated with it. The struggles between France and England, and between England and the United States, occurred in part because of fur-trade rivalry in the Upper Great Lakes, of which the island region was a key section. Industries such as the fur trade, lumbering, and brownstone quarrying flourished there, waned, and all but vanished. Not all ties with the past have been severed, however. Since 1834 commercial fishermen have harvested almost annual catches in the cold waters of Lake Superior around the Apostles. Mining for iron and copper boomed nearby in the nineteenth century, but since has nearly disappeared. Only farming, apple horticulture, and tourism hold much promise, and of them tourism (which began in earnest in the 1890's) alone augurs prosperity for the region called Chequamegon—a name which the tourist often encounters but rarely hears explained.

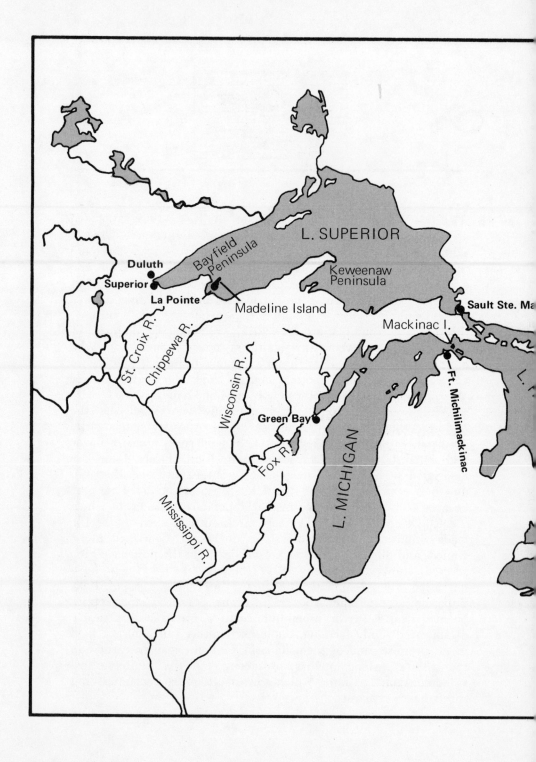

L. SUPERIOR

Bayfield Peninsula

Keweenaw Peninsula

Duluth

Superior

La Pointe

Madeline Island

Sault Ste. Ma

Mackinac I.

St. Croix R.

Chippewa R.

Wisconsin R.

Ft. Michilimackinac

Green Bay

Fox R.

L. MICHIGAN

Mississippi R.

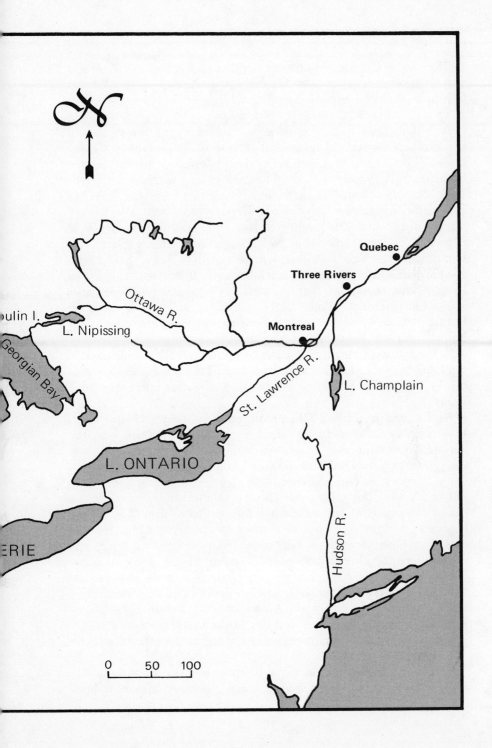

Quebec

Three Rivers

Montreal

Ottawa R.

L. Nipissing

oulin I.

Georgian Bay

L. Champlain

St. Lawrence R.

L. ONTARIO

Hudson R.

ERIE

0   50   100

The name Chequamegon was applied to the region by traders and missionaries soon after its discovery. According to William Whipple Warren, historian of the Chippewa Indians, it derives from a Chippewa (Ojibway) word, *shagwaumikong,* meaning soft beaver dam, and it unintentionally testifies to the abundance of beaver thereabouts and to the importance of the beaver to the fur trade. Two regional landmarks are endowed with the name: Chequamegon Point, the spit of land extending northwesterly into Lake Superior south of Madeline Island and east of Bayfield Peninsula, which the Chippewa believe to have been a legendary beaver dam; and Chequamegon Bay, the entrance to which is bounded by the spit and by Houghton Point on Bayfield Peninsula. The spit formerly was attached to Long Island, but waves and wind wore a channel between them, and the tip of Long Island, though no longer a part of Chequamegon Point, now sports Chequamegon Point Light, a navigational aid. During the French regime Chequamegon Point also was known simply as La Pointe, and La Pointe and Chequamegon became synonyms, not only for the western part of Lake Superior but for the distinctive sand spit as well. The community named La Pointe—successor to earlier villages on Madeline Island—did not come into being until 1834-1835.

As for pronunciation, Chequamegon is a twister. For a time, Wisconsin's radio network used it as an informal test for apprentice announcers. If a novice could slide his tongue around Chequamegon, he could not be stumped. Even so, a choice exists. Some authorities cite nineteenth-century writers who insist it is *she-kwah'-me-gun;* others cite local pronunciation, in which the initial consonant of the second syllable is dropped, and the word becomes *she-wah'-me-gun.* One more troublesome name appears early in Chequamegon's history: Medart Chouart, Sieur des Groseilliers, brother-in-law of the author of the 1659 account, Pierre Esprit Radisson. Locally, the pair is known as Radisson and Groseilliers, pronounced *grow-sell-yours',* and remembered by Anglophiles as "Radishes and Gooseberries." But in French they would have been Radisson and *des* Groseilliers, pronounced *day gro-zay-ayz* without an accented syllable. Either choice can be considered correct.

Although Radisson and Groseilliers were the first definitely recorded white visitors to Chequamegon, they well may have been preceded by others whose identity never may be known because of the lack of records. Scholars are agreed that the most likely candidate for the discovery of Lake Superior is Etienne Brule, but there is outright disagreement about the date and no certain knowledge whether he actually reached the Apostles. One historian puts the date as early as 1615; another, 1618. But the most probable date lies between 1621 and 1623. Two bits of evidence support this conclusion. The first is a 1623 statement by the Recollect missionary and historian Gabriel Sagard that "the interpreter Brusle" and some Indians had assured authorities of the lake's existence. The second is Samuel de Champlain's 1632 map of New France, which shows the lake's size and location approximately and gives a sketchy outline of the south shore. An opposite conclusion argues that Brule merely reached the St. Marys River, and no farther, probably because his Indian companions guarded their knowledge about sources of furs and trading routes.

Brule's discovery was no accident. It resulted from Champlain's policies, as governor of New France, to seek a passage to the Pacific and the Orient, to conduct the fur trade, to discover resources and develop them, to encourage colonization, to locate and Christianize Indians, and to form the institutions of government and civilization. France had known about the St. Lawrence River and its potential for fish and fur ever since Jacques Cartier's exploratory journeys of 1534, 1536, and 1541. But the French could not spare the resources or manpower to act there until relative quiet had been restored in France and Europe, a situation which did not exist until after 1588, with the defeat by the English of the Spanish Armada.

The success of France and Champlain, who made his first journey to the New World in 1603, depended upon co-operation of the Indian population. Indian opposition could well have doomed the settlement. Champlain chose to ally France with the Huron Indians, who controlled access by way of the Ottawa River to the Upper Lakes and their fur treasures. The choice was not popular with tribes that competed with the Huron for the fur trade, and Champlain gave the Huron firearms to fend off the attacking Iroquois, who had more primitive weapons.

To cement Huron-French relations, Champlain in 1609 sent young Frenchmen to live among the Huron, to learn their language, and to become interpreters. Etienne Brule, the first such interpreter, reached Lake Superior by way of a route that was used by traders for nearly 200 years, a series of lakes and streams that led from the St. Lawrence to the Upper Great Lakes—Lakes Michigan, Huron, and Superior. He took the St. Lawrence to the Ottawa River, went west up the Ottawa to its branch, the Mattawa, up the Mattawa, then portaged to Lake Nipissing and paddled down the French River to Georgian Bay of Lake Huron. Even after steam vessels began to ply the Lower Great Lakes, this route remained the speediest but most difficult for men in a hurry to reach the fur depot at Mackinac Island, and it was used well into the nineteenth century. It indicates as well a fact of geography that is crucial to understanding the development of the region: Chequamegon's orientation is east-west, looking towards Canada and the West, not towards the American metropolises to the south and southeast. Even in the twentieth century Chequamegon has kept its back turned on Wisconsin, and its residents feel closer ties to the Michigan-Minnesota neighbors to the east and west than to their fellow Wisconsinites in the south of the state.

As the fur trade burgeoned, the Indians of the Upper Lakes relied more and more upon the goods supplied them by whites: cooking utensils, weapons, clothing, ornaments and jewelry, blankets, and liquor. In their eagerness to acquire articles of a manufacturing economy, the Indians rapidly harvested fur-bearing animals in areas convenient to Quebec, where Champlain founded a city and erected a stockade in 1608. The depleted supply forced them to search further.

A similar situation existed south and east of Quebec where the shortage pressed the Iroquois—five allied nations sometimes called the Iroquois Confederacy, who traded mostly with the British and Dutch. The Iroquois controlled the fur trade along the Hudson River and into western New York. (The Huron—chief competitors to the confederacy—actually were a sixth tribe of Iroquoian stock, but were not, thanks to their commercial ties to the French, included in the arrangement.) Finally, goaded to their limit by Huron control over the essential Ottawa River fur-trade route, the Iroquois in 1648 swept into Huron villages and laid them waste. The survivors scattered, some retreating to Quebec, most fleeing north and west, accompanied by friendly Ottawa bands. Iroquois depredations continued, until by 1658 the Huron had retreated as far west as a six days' journey south of Lake Superior, where Radisson and Groseilliers visited them.

Sioux Indians, who occupied much of Minnesota and part of western Wisconsin, resented these encroachments, and the Huron and Ottawa moved again, this time to Chequamegon. In about 1670, the Sioux forced the tribes east, the Ottawa to Manitoulin Island in Lake Huron and the Huron to Michilimackinac (now Mackinaw City, Michigan).

THE Iroquois menace redistributed Indians throughout Wisconsin. In addition to forcing the Huron and Ottawa to Chequamegon, the Iroquois forced the Chippewa to move from the vicinity to Sault Ste. Marie westward, both north and south of Lake Superior. From 1680 onward, it would appear, the Chippewa dominated Chequamegon. When and where they lived on Madeline Island still is, unfortunately, a matter of conjecture and some disagreement. William Whipple Warren, who defined Chequamegon, wrote an account of the Chippewa in 1852 based upon their oral history, which he had learned as a well-educated member of a prominent Madeline Island fur-trading family of mixed Chippewa and white blood. Warren stated that the Chippewa lived on the island from 1490 to about 1630, when they were forced towards Sault Ste. Marie by marauding Sioux. He related further that Chippewa would not dwell overnight on Madeline Island without French or British protection until well into the nineteenth century. Modern historians and anthropologists dispute Warren, citing reports of seventeenth-century missionaries and explorers to the effect that the Chippewa lived on Madeline from about 1680 onward. They believe that Chippewa legend errs in its chronology, and that Warren's statements about the early village apply to the historic, late-seventeenth-century settlement.

No archeological evidence has been uncovered to support either view. That such evidence exists cannot be doubted, but securing permission from private owners to dig for it and securing the funds for such research complicate matters. A further complication is the attitude of the Chippewa themselves. Traditionally they have resented tampering with the graves of

13

their ancestors. In 1916, when a young anthropologist appeared on the island, he was informed that local Indians would resist him forcibly should he attempt any digging whatever, even excluding graves. Further, the most likely sites were beneath cornfields, and the island farmers and gardeners were ill-disposed to permit a youthful scholar to ruin their crops. In the end he merely recommended excavating sites in a mile-wide band stretching across the island from Kapunky or Sunset Bay on the west to Chebomnicon Bay on the east, where the Chippewa village supposedly existed from about 1680 onward, and also at the supposed sites of the various forts and fur company quarters.

Only one systematic archeological dig has been conducted on the island, although a great many artifacts have been unearthed by a talented amateur anthropologist and island resident, Al Galazen. Parts of both collections are in the Madeline Island Historical Museum. In the summer of 1961 a dig was conducted near Grant's Point on the southwestern shore, where were found remains of a long rectangular Indian dwelling, pottery sherds, stone arrowheads and other Indian-made articles, and some European trade goods. These artifacts were examined by another anthropologist, who has decided they are remains of a Huron settlement, dating between 1650 and 1670, when the Huron definitely lived in the area. Early articles found by Galazen include an elbow pipe made of fired clay in typical Huron style, but decorated with the head of a pig, whose snout appears clearly. The French introduced pigs to the Huron between ´1630 and 1650, and the Huron quickly added the animal to their series of effigy pipes, which included human heads and bear heads as well.

Articles in the museum which date from a much later period—1760 to 1820—were also unearthed by Galazen. These include silver ornaments made exclusively for Indian trade by Canadian silversmiths, parts of guns, bits of English pottery, pewter tableware, jackknives, scissors, nails, white kaolin pipes, strike-a-lights, glass bottles, and so on—all trade articles. Items made by Indians include a tip of a birchbark canoe, an etching of a ship on birchbark, and some pipes. Survival of the birchbark underground has been attributed to the presence of water only a few feet below the surface. Birchbark disintegrates in soil but survives in water, to which it is impervious. Birchbark containers can hold and boil water, but Indians quickly discarded them when brass and iron kettles became available. The artifacts' survival depended, too, on a geological phenomenon, which has raised the island's water table. Geologists say that the north shore of Lake Superior is rising, as it has been for thousands of years. As it tilts upward, the southern shore and Madeline Island tilt downward, so that areas that were dry 300 years ago are now submerged or marshy. Hence the survival of the birchbark.

To date no articles have been found on the island which can be associated with the years 1670-1760. Because the French occupied Madeline almost uninterruptedly during that span, rich archeological sites assuredly exist. Again, none has been excavated.

Iroquois predatoriness led the Huron to abandon the fur trade altogether, leaving the remains to the Ottawa, and by 1653 the trade had dwindled to nothing. Not a single beaver skin was received that year by the warehouses in Montreal, which had replaced Quebec as fur headquarters in 1642, the year it was founded. A truce with the Iroquois prompted resumption of the trade in 1654, but with a twist designed to reduce Indian control. Instead of relying upon Indians to act as middlemen, the French sent their own traders along with the Indians to find furs and bring them to Montreal. Ultimately this change in French tactics led to settlement of the West.

One of the first two French traders under the new system was Groseilliers, forty-six years old in 1654. In that year, he and an unknown companion (not Radisson, contrary to his own account) scoured the Lake region and bought enough furs to revive the sagging Montreal economy. Groseilliers together with Radisson then sought a license for a second trip. French officials agreed to grant it only if civil and church authorities accompanied the traders. The demand coincided with a major missionary movement under the Jesuits in New France, beginning in 1632. The Jesuits reasoned that the fur trade would introduce them to the Indians they ardently desired to convert, so they abetted the trade, and by the middle 1600's controlled perhaps 90 per cent of it in New France.

Radisson and Groseilliers resisted the government's demands and left secretly for Lake Superior. Once there they portaged across the Keweenaw Peninsula, using a well-worn path that they

15

found. In the fall of 1659 they reached Chequamegon Bay and built a cabin, the site of which is not known, but which may have been on Whittlesey Creek. Indians greeted the traders warmly, since they already had been exposed to trade goods. According to Radisson: "We weare Cesars, being nobody to contradict us. We went away free from any burden, whilst those poore miserable thought themselves happy to carry our Equipage, for the hope that they had that we should give them a brasse ring, or an awle, or an needle." The men cached their goods and made their way into the interior to winter among Huron, Ottawa, and Chippewa Indians. While staying with Ottawa, probably near Lac Court Oreilles, they nearly starved. They ate dogs, then bones, and even filthy beaver skins, becoming "the very image of death." Conditions eventually eased, hunting became possible, and a feast was served for eighteen bands of Indians. On their return to the bay, the two explorers built a "fort," probably on the end of Chequamegon Point.

Radisson and Groseilliers returned to the St. Lawrence in 1660 with a harvest of furs that again snatched the colony from the brink of economic ruin. In punishment for their unauthorized departure, the governor of New France fined the two men, confiscated all but $20,000 worth of furs, reserved at least five times that amount for New France, and jailed Groseilliers. Despite all this, the traders again sought a license, this time to trade in the Hudson's Bay area, about which they had learned from some Indians. Authorities both in New France and France spurned their petitions, so the two turned to New England and were spurned again. Even French merchants refused support. Finally after nearly a decade of negotiations, they succeeded in interesting parties in England who, on May 2, 1670, were chartered as the Hudson's Bay Company, a firm which harried New France for decades.

A Jesuit missionary, Father Rene Menard, set out for Chequamegon the year that Radisson and Groseilliers returned with their unlicensed trove of furs. The veteran missionary priest cajoled his way with traders and Ottawa tribesmen so that he could minister to Indian refugees near Madeline Island, but his health failed and the weather turned against him, forcing him to winter at Keweenaw Bay in Upper Michigan, where, it is said, he was badly treated by the traders, who resented his interference with the Indians. In the spring, before the ice left western Lake Superior, Father Menard was summoned by some half-starved Huron Indians at the headwaters of the Black River. On his way to them, he strayed into the forest while his French guide maneuvered their canoe through a difficult rapids, thought to be the dells of the Big Rib River in southeastern Taylor and southwestern Lincoln counties of Wisconsin. His body was never found, although his breviary and cassock were discovered on a Sioux altar years later. A great deal of disagreement and speculation exist about Father Menard's journey and place of death, but it is almost certain that he never reached Chequamegon Bay, his destination.

The next appointed missionary did reach Chequamegon. He was Father Claude Allouez, a Jesuit, appointed in 1663 as the vicar general of the interior. On August 8, 1665, Allouez left Three Rivers, Quebec, for Chequamegon, accompanied by six traders and more than 400 Indians, most of whom dropped out along the way. Allouez found an Ottawa settlement at Fish Creek and a Huron settlement at what is now Bono's Creek. Allouez built a birchbark chapel between the two Indian villages, probably on Boyd Creek. He had expected that the Indians would have retained some of the Christian teachings they had learned in the East before they fled the Iroquois, but he was mistaken. He had to begin anew and he enjoyed few successes. Accordingly he moved his mission—called La Pointe de Saint Esprit (Mission of the Holy Spirit)—to the Ottawa village proper. Again he met failure, and some angry Ottawa burned his tiny chapel, from which Allouez barely escaped alive. The missionary decided he needed more help, and he left for Quebec on May 6, 1667, completing the circumnavigation of Lake Superior on his way, the first white man of record to do so.

Allouez recruited aides in Quebec, only to have them refused passage by *coureurs de bois,* a French term which translates "wood runners." They were laborers for the fur traders and their companies, and the descriptive term for them, frequently taken as a pejorative, actually applied to nearly everyone engaged in the fur trade apart from administrators and missionaries. One priest made the trip with Allouez, but he proved nearly useless at Chequamegon, owing to his abhorrence of pagans and of hardships, so he gave up and went to Quebec when Lake

17

Superior's ice broke up. Allouez lingered at Chequamegon, having found the Indians eager to be baptized, and later in 1668 he left, promising to send another missionary.

One of the most famous missionaries in all of North American history, Father Jacques Marquette, replaced him, but experienced difficulty at Chequamegon. Sioux Indians harassed him and the Ottawa and Huron among whom he worked, and in 1671 Marquette left for Sault Ste. Marie with a band of the faithful. Missionaries did not appear again in Chequamegon until the early 1800's. Marquette, on June 17, 1673, discovered the Upper Mississippi River, the achievement for which he is most noted.

No traces of Allouez and Marquette's missions remain. Their tiny chapels were destroyed, and the sites upon which they stood never have been found. Nonetheless, nineteenth-century tourist guidebooks instructed travelers to Madeline Island to inspect Marquette's chapel at La Pointe (in reality an 1841 mission church) and a rather ordinary copy of Reubens' "Descent from the Cross," which the guidebook attributed to Reubens himself. Delighted Americans gobbled up the story, and a convention boatload of Wisconsin editors eagerly disseminated the tale throughout the state in their weekly sheets.

THE next recorded French visitor at Chequamegon was Daniel Greysolon Dulhut, for whom the Minnesota city at the tip of Lake Superior is named Duluth. Dulhut set out from Montreal on September 1, 1678, as the representative of Quebec and Montreal merchants who had received a charter for an exploration and trading company from the head of New France, which in 1663 under Louis XIV had become a royal rather than a privately administered colony. By the 1670's the new arrangement had resulted in soaring profits from the fur trade, and it was decided to send French traders to deal directly with the Sioux Indians, who had access to the richest fur territories. Dulhut was such a trader. He achieved astonishing successes on his journey. Near the city named for him, he conducted a peace council between the Sioux and Chippewa and induced them to accept a truce. He spent the winter of 1679-1680 on Chequamegon Bay, where he made friends with Indians, among whom were some who had returned from Sault Ste. Marie to which they had fled during Marquette's missionary tenure.

The decade 1680-1690 brought few changes to Chequamegon, while elsewhere in Wisconsin the fur trade expanded, as it did south of the Great Lakes. The French, because of their expansionist tendencies, were besieged by both Indians and the British. The western tribes especially had begun to favor British traders, since English goods and English prices were better than those of the French, who frequently demanded twice as many beaver pelts as their enemies for guns, powder, and blankets. The Iroquois defeated the French in four battles during the decade, and only the presence of French militia, and the friendship of men like Dulhut with the Indians, enabled them to retain their trade advantage. King William's war with England, which began in 1689, worsened matters, and at war's end in 1697 France was fortunate to keep her fur territories.

Dulhut had special difficulties with the Sioux at Chequamegon, pressed as he was by the incursions of British traders from the north. About 1690—the date is not certain—he moved his headquarters from the head of Lake Superior to the Chequamegon Point, an easily defended site. Then, in 1693, the Comte de Frontenac, governor of New France, replaced Dulhut with Pierre Le Sueur as commander of a detail of soldiers and as chief of traders.

Le Sueur chose as his fort site a spot near the southern tip of Madeline Island, probably along what is now the western shore and very near Grant's Point, called Moningwana Nei-asha—golden-breasted woodpecker point—by the Chippewa in recognition of the many flickers or golden-breasted woodpeckers on the island. In the seventeenth century, the western shore of the island extended perhaps 1,000 feet further into the channel that it does at present, and the fort backed on a lagoon which has filled in.

Le Sueur extended efforts well beyond the island, and furs consequently funneled to it from the south and west, and even from the east, the pelts from eastern trappers coming by way of the Fox-Wisconsin waterway. The waterway's outlet to Lake Michigan through Green Bay had been sealed by English and Indian forces, so the French turned northwest to Chequamegon.

Madeline Island's heyday under Le Sueur was short-lived. He and other traders and unlicensed coureurs de bois were so

19

successful in gathering furs that they glutted the market, which fell to disastrous levels. In March, 1696, Louis XIV consequently cancelled all trade licenses and forbade further shipments of trade goods to remote areas. News traveled slowly, and it was not until 1698 that Le Sueur abandoned the island.

Louis XIV intended to restore the trade to its previous basis, when Indians brought furs to the French rather than having traders go among the Indians, but he and Frontenac failed to obey their own designs. Both permitted some trading to continue, in part because of the persistent threat of English competition and because of continued military difficulties with England (Queen Anne's War) and with the Fox Indians, who fought two unsuccessful wars, ending in 1738, in an attempt to create a pan-Indian economic movement. As these developments matured, the French reversed their earlier decision and again arranged to send licensed traders into the wilderness to secure forts, rather than relying upon Indian initiative. By 1717, the policy had been reinstated completely, and in 1718 the French reactivated their fort on Madeline Island, calling it Fort La Pointe.

The new commander chose a different site for the fort, along the western shore on what is now called Sandy Bay. It stood somewhere south of the Indian Cemetery near the present marina. Its precise outlines are not known, but some objects have been retrieved from the sandy soil in the area. Later residents called this installation Middle Fort, presumably because it stood between the later Protestant Mission House site and the American Fur Company quarters.

A succession of French commanders had charge of the area, one of the most important being Louis Denis, Sieur de la Ronde, who with his son and wife dominated affairs at Chequamegon from about 1727 through 1748. The elder La Ronde established agriculture on the island, spurred the fur trade, and attempted to develop a copper mining industry. In 1733 La Ronde drew the king's attention to the masses of free copper on what is now Michigan's Upper Peninsula and on the Lake Superior islands. He proposed developing the deposits at his own expense, in exchange for nine years' control of the island post, for which office he would not be charged the usual fee. La Ronde offered to build two vessels, one for Lake Superior and another for Lake Huron,

20

to ship the copper to civilization. The court accepted the proposal, and La Ronde actually did build one vessel at the Sault. Rigging and metal outfittings of the 25-ton ship were transported by canoe from eastern cities, and the hull was assembled at the Sault. In 1738, two German miners arrived and satisfied themselves that the deposits were more than superficial. Plans proceeded, but they were interrupted by the warring Sioux and Chippewa. La Ronde settled the Indian dispute, then attempted to renew interest in the mines by traveling to Quebec. On his return to the Upper Lakes he fell ill and traveled again to Quebec where he died in 1741. His son and his wife succeeded him. The vessel built by La Ronde may have survived and have been used on Lake Superior until 1763, when a French ship is known to have foundered in its waters. There are no certain records about its fate.

During the La Ronde tenure the name "Apostle Islands" became official, despite the obvious fact that more than a dozen islands exist in the group. In 1973, twenty-two islands were recognized, although some count twenty-three by including Little Manitou Island. Older residents remember a twenty-fourth, Steamboat Island, which gradually wore away. A series of shoals indicates that there may have been still more islands, but at no time were there only twelve. The name Apostle Islands very likely arose from the French habit of assigning names of religious significance to geographic locations, and it may not have been intended to signify a specific number. Despite its numerical inaccuracy, the name stuck. Efforts by the explorer-scientist Henry R. Schoolcraft failed to change it. In 1820 he proposed calling them the Federation Islands, giving each island the name of a state. His proposal failed. Local residents confuse matters by calling some islands what they please. For example, Hermit Island is known as Wilson's, and Stockton is Presque Isle (pronounced *pressk-eel*). The French, too, had special names for specific islands, but they escaped current usage. The most variously named island was Madeline. The French at one time or another called it Isle Detour, Montreal, St. Michael's, La Pointe, St. Esprit, Michel, and La Ronde—for the powerful copper promoter. English names included Cadotte, Woodpecker, Yellow Hammer, Middle, La Pointe, and spelling variants of Madeline, who was the wife of Michel Cadotte, a late-eighteenth-century

21

settler and fur trader from whose time continuous white settlement dates.

La Ronde's successor at La Pointe represented another powerful family of New France—the Marins. Pierre Paul Marin, the father, had been prominent in the West since 1727 and had acquired a reputation for dealing skillfully with Indians, especially the difficult Sioux. His son succeeded Madame La Ronde at La Pointe in 1749, but he remained there only one season, then took over his father's Green Bay position. Records of the Marins' dealings detail the profitableness of the fur trade. During the three years the younger Marin was in charge at Green Bay he and his partner are believed to have made between $62,000 and $125,000. Profits like these made the Marins rich, but wrought a hardship on the mother country, which subsidized the trade by financing operations in New France. Madeline Island accounted for a smaller share of business in New France than other outposts. A sketchy summary for France's last year in the Upper Lakes wilderness, 1759-1760, shows total sales of 1,150,000 *livres* of merchandise, with La Pointe accounting for 80,000 *livres,* compared to Green Bay with 100,000, Mackinac with 250,000, and Detroit with 350,000 *livres,* a single *livre* being worth between 20 and 40 cents.

The younger Marin's successor at La Pointe represented another of New France's most powerful families, the La Verendryes. They had been familiar with the region west of Lake Superior for more than a generation by the time that Jospeh Gaultier, Chevalier de la Verendrye, assumed command of Chequamegon in 1751. His father had been granted a monopoly over trade in the far west in 1731, and he and his three sons and a nephew traveled as far as Lake Winnipeg and perhaps the Rockies. The territories claimed by the Marin and La Verendrye families overlapped, and the two inevitably squabbled about profits.

La Verendrye's departure from La Pointe and the acknowledged outbreak of war between Britain and France on the North American continent coincided in 1755-1756. The conflict, called the French and Indian War in the United States and the Seven Years' War in Europe, involved both Indians and Frenchmen from Chequamegon. La Verendrye's successor left La Pointe in 1758 with a detachment of Indian troops and fought

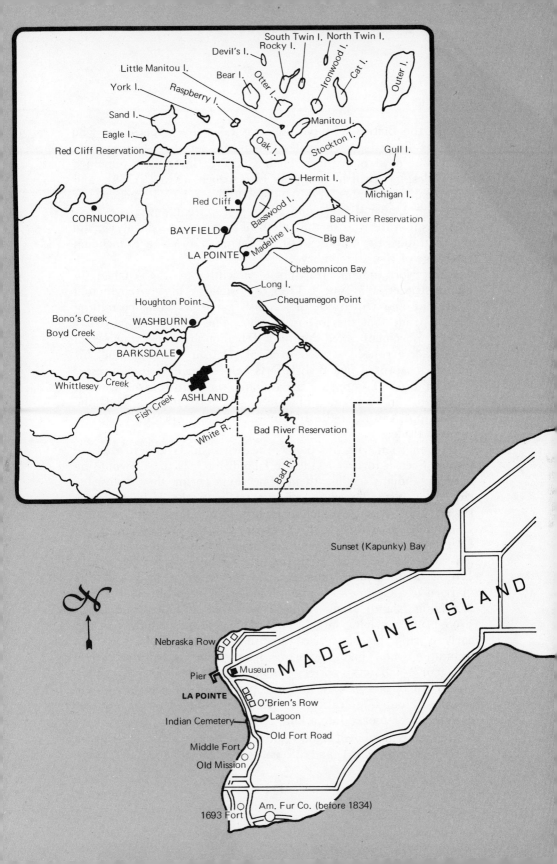

South Twin I.
North Twin I.
Rocky I.
Devil's I.
Little Manitou I.
Bear I.
Otter I.
Ironwood I.
Cat I.
Outer I.
York I.
Raspberry I.
Sand I.
Manitou I.
Eagle I.
Oak I.
Stockton I.
Red Cliff Reservation
Gull I.
Hermit I.
CORNUCOPIA
Red Cliff
Michigan I.
Basswood I.
Bad River Reservation
BAYFIELD
Madeline I.
Big Bay
LA POINTE
Chebomnicon Bay
Long I.
Houghton Point
Chequamegon Point
Bono's Creek
WASHBURN
Boyd Creek
BARKSDALE
Whittlesey Creek
ASHLAND
Fish Creek
White R.
Bad River Reservation
Bad R.

Sunset (Kapunky) Bay

MADELINE ISLAND

Nebraska Row
Museum
Pier
LA POINTE
O'Brien's Row
Indian Cemetery
Lagoon
Old Fort Road
Middle Fort
Old Mission
Am. Fur Co. (before 1834)
1693 Fort

against the British. His position was taken by a speculator who paid the French government 8,000 francs for the Chequamegon lease. The new commander, Sieur Corne de la St. Luc, remained there despite British conquest of Quebec (May, 1759) and Montreal (September, 1760), the withdrawal of French troops from the Upper Lakes, and a French retreat down the Fox-Wisconsin waterway to the safety of French Louisiana. He did not relinquish the outpost until the spring of 1762—a Frenchman in charge of British territory.

Chippewa Indians responded violently to the change in administration. On June 4, 1763, they staged a bloody rebellion at Mackinac and wiped out the British garrison, while permitting French traders at the fort to survive. The revolt was part of a general movement called Pontiac's Rebellion after an Ottawa chief who had arranged a take-over at Detroit. Pontiac and his followers captured five British forts before the British suppressed them in 1764. To appease the Indians, the British forbade white settlement in a region between the Alleghenies and the Mississippi, calling it the Indian Reserve and opening it only to licensed traders.

In connection with this policy, the British in 1765 destroyed the former French fort on Madeline Island, for fear that it would be used by Indians against them. The same spring they licensed a citizen of New Jersey to conduct trade in the Lake Superior region. He was Alexander Henry, who had sent men to Chequamegon as early as 1761. Henry had been raised among the Chippewa and had narrowly escaped death in the Mackinac massacre. He selected Jean Baptiste Cadotte as his partner in 1765. Cadotte's father had come to the Sault in 1671 and was married to a Chippewa woman, and their descendants still live on Madeline Island. Henry himself wintered at Chequamegon in 1765-1766, surviving largely on Lake Superior whitefish. In the early spring he supervised manufacture of maple sugar, a technique he had learned from the Chippewa. His voyageurs—laborers, porters, boatmen—ate less grandly. Each received a bushel of corn and two pounds of fat a month—their so-called "found" or ration—to which they added water and fish or game to be cooked into a kind of gruel.

Henry accumulated 15,000 pounds of beaver skins (150 packs at 100 pounds each) and 25 packs of marten and otter skins during the season and this success fostered continued activity in Chequamegon. In 1767, eighteen canoes carrying £7,481 of trade goods left trading headquarters at Mackinac for Chequamegon. Trade continued to go well, and in 1774 the British attached the entire region from Quebec to the Mississippi and Ohio rivers to Quebec Province for administrative purposes. The realignment angered the English colonies in the east, since they had had some jurisdiction over western fur trade, but it pleased the Montreal merchants. The enlarged Quebec Province helped goad potential American revolutionaries and therefore contributed to the outbreak of the Revolutionary War.

THE Revolution, however, little affected Chequamegon. If anything, it improved trade there by diverting British attention from the fur fields in the war zone to the south towards Lake Superior and its relatively untapped fur resources. Grand Portage, Minnesota, at the Canadian border on Lake Superior, became the point of access to the regions of Lake of the Woods and Lake Winnipeg, and eventually to the fur territories on the Pacific coast. The Montreal merchants experienced their best years on record during the bloodiest years of the British-American conflict. In 1778 the British licensed 152 canoes and 374 bateaux for Lake Superior posts, carrying goods worth £191,013, the best year for trade during the war. At war's end, British figures indicated fur shipments nearly identical to those recorded at the war's beginning.

Wisconsin's Indian population exhibited mixed feelings about the war. Some supported the British, some the revolutionaries. At the end of the war the British surrendered to the new United States all territory west to the Mississippi and along the present Canadian border, including Chequamegon, and Chequamegon became American in name, though in fact it was still allied geographically and ethnically with Canada and its French and British fur traders.

Montreal merchants easily retained their grip on Chequamegon's trade. The 1783 Treaty of Paris required the British to relinquish their forts "with all convenient speed," but the inconvenience of losing the fur trade slowed the British to a crawl. The Americans, occupied with numerous problems, moved slowly themselves in cementing relations with the Indians around Lake Superior. In August, 1787, the Canadian government prolonged foreign involvement on American soil by organizing a council with most of Wisconsin's tribes, including the Chippewa. They agreed to acknowledge England's king as their ruler, and Lake Superior became "a British pond."

Between 1780 and 1790, trade in the western Lake Superior region and beyond increased in importance because heavy settlement to the east decimated the animal population. The value of the furs taken from Mackinac and west was £89,000 in 1780 and £104,400 in 1790. The North West Company, formed probably as early as 1779, began to dominate in Chequamegon. At first Alexander Henry did not join. In 1782 he sent Michel Cadotte, son of his partner, to trade independently in the region. Then, in 1787, Henry did join the North West Company, along with other small operators, and he brought the Cadottes with him.

The large Montreal operators agitated throughout the decade for removal of licensing restrictions on the fur trade and for establishing an open market. In 1791 the government capitulated, and more small trading outfits succumbed. That same year the North West Company established an Irish trader, John Johnston, on Madeline Island. Independent trappers tried to force Johnston from the region, but did not succeed, and in 1793 he married the daughter of a Chippewa chief.

Johnston reported that he found the Apostles "a rich soil covered with maple and beech, with deep water and fine trout fishing." His description varies somewhat with later ones, which emphasized the prevalence of pine, which, together with maple and hemlock, prevails still. (Johnston was no doubt right, because the island has a longer growing season than nearby mainland areas where pine alone predominates. Madeline Island has a growing season of 150 days; the area along the eastern shore of the Bayfield Peninsula has a season of 130 days; and ten miles inland the season's length declines to 115 days.)

The year of Johnston's marriage, 1793, was a year of significance for the island generally, for it marked permanent settlement. The settler was Michel Cadotte, who was appointed there by the North West Company. Cadotte was married to a daughter of Chief White

Crane, hereditary Chippewa leader there. She was baptized at the time of their wedding and her name was changed from Equaysayway, Traveling Woman, to the Christian name Madeleine. White Crane bestowed the name as well upon the island. Its spelling has been altered slightly since then.

Cadotte established quarters on the southern shore of the island, very near the commemorative plaque on a granite boulder on the west side of Old Fort Road, and the island once again assumed importance as a fur depot. The North West Company made it a trading center for Chequamegon, balanced by another at Fond du Lac at the western end of Lake Superior. The company's buildings sprang up slightly to the east of Cadotte's cabin, and as many as eight dwellings were reported to have stood there. The North West Company, which one disgruntled competitor dubbed "Legislator and King," easily dominated the trade in the Upper Lakes and to the west, absorbing competing firms and solidly establishing itself.

At about the same time, American traders began to appear along the Upper Lakes. Their arrival resulted from Jay's Treaty of 1795, between England and the United States, in which the new nation pledged neutrality in the strife with France and Spain, and England in turn withdrew from military posts along the American side of the Great Lakes. The withdrawal was nominal, since the British merely established new posts on the Canadian side and continued to trade with United States Indians. The American response to these and other British maneuvers led ultimately to the involvement of John Jacob Astor in the fur trade and to the development of Madeline Island as one of the key fur stations in the country.

To protect American fur trade, Congress imposed high tariffs on all foreign goods, including the trade articles that came from Canada and England for sale to Indian fur trappers in American territory. To circumvent the tariffs, the North West Company in 1806 contracted with an American firm for American operation of all North West posts east of the Mississippi. Michel Cadotte remained in charge at Madeline and a Scotsman supervised at Mackinac, where he smuggled goods past American inspectors and avoided duties.

In 1811 officials of the North West Company devised another

scheme to evade import taxes. It combined with its American agent, the Michilimackinac Company, and with John Jacob Astor of New York to form the South West Company, so named because it would handle trade south and west of the Canadian border. Astor, as an American, legitimatized the concern for tax purposes. Astor was no stranger to the fur trade. During the Napoleonic Wars he had shipped North West Company furs in his vessels to England, so the furs could pass French warships unmolested. In 1808 he incorporated the American Fur Company under the laws of New York State, in hopes of monopolizing the trade on the entire North American continent. In time, Astor's name became synonymous with fur trade and especially with the beaver, despite his involvements in real estate, finance, and general mercantilism. (Astor and the poetically appropriate castor [beaver] are paired today in the New York City subway system, which has marked the Astor Place station on the Lexington Avenue line with terra cotta reliefs of a beaver gnawing on a tree.)

Astor's European customers demanded the beaver skin above all others because its soft underhairs could be compressed into a stiff fabric perfect for making tophats. In the 1830's, with a change in fashion and technology and a decline in the population of the overhunted beaver, the raccoon replaced the beaver as the most hunted animal. By 1850 the beaver skin stood fifth in total number of skins exported, trailing the raccoon, muskrat, mink, and fox.

Astor especially must have coveted the trade from around Lake Superior. Furs from that territory were among the best in America, owing to the long winters and dense forests. The winters produced thick, lush pelts. The forests provided ample winter food and healthy animals. But Astor was frustrated until 1815 in his hopes to acquire the Lake Superior and Chequamegon trade. The War of 1812 kept Lake Superior a British pond. The British took and held Fort Mackinac in July, 1812, and rebuffed Americans there in 1814. Throughout, they clung to the fur trade. Finally, with the Treaty of Ghent on December 24, 1814, the British agreed to withdraw to Canadian territory and to open the Upper Lakes to American traders.

Astor quickly capitalized on this opportunity. He renewed the South West Company agreement in 1816, and he insisted upon a clause that would have rendered the contract void if the U.S. Congress were to bar foreigners from trading in furs within its jurisdiction. Congress, under pressure applied by Astor, voted in the magnate's favor on April 29, 1816. The vote gave Astor a toehold on Madeline Island where Cadotte remained as factor—the person in charge of the fur factory or warehouse-trading post. American Fur Company field operations were headed by Ramsay Crooks, who became a familiar figure on the island, assisted by Robert Stuart, both Scotsmen with years of experience in the fur trade. They had trekked overland to Astoria, Oregon, on Astor's famous expedition of 1812-1813, and they were intimate with both hardship and profit margins.

The American Fur Company dominated in Chequamegon, but did not monopolize the trade there, or anywhere in the West. Beyond the Upper Mississippi, the Hudson's Bay Company and the North West Company battled for control and extended their operations to American soil. To the south Astor faced competition from publicly owned U.S. government fur factories, which the country relinquished in 1823 under further pressure applied by Astor and other giants of the fur trade.

Among the independents who traded in Chequamegon were Lyman Marcus Warren and Truman Warren, brothers from New England who arrived at Lac du Flambeau and Lac Court Oreilles in 1818. They prospered and moved to Madeline Island, where they met and were married in 1821 to daughters of Michel Cadotte, the factor. Two years later they bought Cadotte's interests and Lyman became factor in 1824. He eventually came to own a one-twelfth interest in the Northern Outfit of the firm and some stock in the parent company itself.

Under Warren, the island acquired some cultural refinements and religious and educational institutions, all of which usually followed soon after New Englanders transplanted themselves to the western wilderness. Similar invasions swept southern Wisconsin throughout the late 1830's and 1840's as civilization marched into the state. For years, well into the 1850's, La Pointe—by then the little village on Madeline—alone in the northwestern corner of the state boasted such accouterments. The first missionary-teacher was sent in 1827, but got only as far as Mackinac, where he was persuaded to remain. In 1830, Frederick Ayer, a teacher at Mackinac, came to Madeline at Warren's behest and started a school for the Warren offspring and the children of Indians on the island, of whom there were about 200. On August 30, 1831, the Reverend Sherman Hall, a Presbyterian missionary from Vermont, arrived under the auspices of the American Board of Commissioners for Foreign Missions, which worked among American Indians as well as abroad. Hall's journals and letters provide an excellent description of life at La Pointe and in northwest Wisconsin for a span of twenty-three years—the period of the island's greatest importance and growth.

From Hall, for example, come specifications for birchbark canoes and bateaux, which were giant cargo canoes that measured forty or fifty feet in length, ten to twelve feet amidships, and required a crew of at least six or seven hardy oarsmen. Passengers sat precariously and uncomfortably atop the five tons of cargo that each bateau could carry. On his progress with the Indians: "We are barbarians to the Indians, and they to us." And, "Their ideas of a Supreme Being seem to be vague and indistinct. Yet they acknowledge a Great Spirit who made them." On the dress of voyageurs: "short shirt, a red woollen cap, a pair of deer skin moccasins without stockings on the feet. The thighs are left bare. This is the dress of voyageurs in summer and winter, and is substantially the common dress of the Indians." Voyageurs, he wrote, toted their loads overland when necessary by means of a strap around the forehead, attached to thongs that secured the load to their backs. The voyageur then walked bent over, and in this uncomfortable position could heft 400 to 500 pounds and carry the load for a thousand yards. Hall found forty or fifty acres under cultivation on the southeastern tip of the island, and he reported the existence of the various buildings associated with a small village and trading post.

WITHIN a few years of Hall's arrival, events within the American Fur Company triggered changes that completely altered the company and the appearance of the island. In 1834, Astor divided his company in half. He sold the Western Department with offices at St. Louis to the famous fur-trading enterprise of Pratt, Chouteau and Company. He sold the other half, the Northern Department, to Crooks and his associates for $300,000. Crooks kept the name of the firm, the American Fur Company.

These internal realignments forced Crooks to re-evaluate and adjust the field operations of the Northern Department with an eye towards making them more profitable. Sometime before 1834, Madeline Island had been made headquarters for the Northern Outfit, which answered to the Northern Department at Mackinac. The outfit consisted of eleven sub-outfits. After 1834, Crooks reduced Mackinac's status to that of a way station and replaced it with La Pointe in order to cut shipping expenses. Most of the goods distributed to the Lake Superior region formerly had been rowed in clumsy forty-foot boats to the falls of St. Mary's, then were portaged and rowed again over treacherous Lake Superior. Crooks decided to build a 112-ton schooner for Lake Superior, the *John Jacob Astor,* to ease half the tedious journey, and another schooner, the *Ramsay Crooks,* to sail in Lakes Michigan and Huron. The boatmen thus freed from rowing were to become fishermen in the fur company's employ, and they too were to operate from La Pointe. Crooks feared that if a fishing operation were not created, the discharged boatmen would join rival fur traders. He also reduced the number of La Pointe sub-outfits from eleven to nine. His decisions rendered La Pointe an administrative, fishing, and warehousing center for the entire Lake Superior and Upper Mississippi region.

No matter where the field headquarters, the company's New York office realized a 5 per cent profit and undertook little risk, which ultimately rested on the shoulders of the men in the woods—the traders who went among the Indians and bartered goods for the Indians furs. If they failed, they could owe the Northern Outfit more furs than they collected. Indians, too, assumed financial responsibilities. Traders extended them credit in advance of receiving furs, knowing that the government would reimburse the company when tribes sold their lands. Often so many claims were placed against a tribe's government receipts that individual Indians received nothing whatever, except reduced mobility, independence, and property. The system profited American Fur Company stockholders. Between 1835 and 1838 the company paid dividends totaling 50 per cent, despite significant losses by its Western Outfit in 1836 and 1837 and by the Sioux Outfit in 1837, as well as small losses at La Pointe, owing to mismanagement by Warren. The profits came from government monies.

Crooks' decisions to enlarge Madeline Island's fur trade role required a change in the location of the post on the island. Historically, the trading colony had occupied the island's southeastern tip. But the tip was exposed to heavy winds from the east and it possessed no adequate harbor. Fortunately, the island has a splendid harbor on its western shore, with sandy beaches and the width of the island behind it and the width of the Bayfield Peninsula before it to buffer Lake Superior storms. The village was moved there, where it remains today.

Missionary Hall moved first. In the fall of 1834 he began building his mission structure about midway between the present La Pointe wharf, which is used by Bayfield-La Pointe ferries, and the southern tip of the island. In February, 1835, the fur company itself began building operations, and by August some of the structures were occupied. Little remains from this village; even the street pattern has been changed. But the wharf, much reduced from its 400-foot length in the halcyon fur-trade days, is in precisely the same location. By 1840, La Pointe exuded an air of prosperity. Charles W. Penny, who accompanied the famed geologist Douglass Houghton on a survey in 1840, reported that the American Fur Company had painted its store and warehouse red and its four or five clapboarded dwellings white. (One of the company's warehouses, now paintless and weathered, is part of the Madeline Island Historical Museum.) Penny found the wharf, with a fish storage house in the middle, to be 250 feet long. He noted that forty-six voyageurs had built dwellings and that about forty Indian lodges stood in the immediate area, "which all together give it the appearance of quite a town."

Life on the island was not without its amenities. The former factor, Lyman Warren, had collected a "large and select library" and subscribed to New York journals, which kept him abreast of contemporary affairs and thought. Warren's successor also had a taste for the finer things. He imported a piano and hired a Scottish governess for his children. The Indians led a simpler existence, but one no less interesting to Penny. On a Sunday he visited Indian lodges. "The girls with bead pantalets, porcupine moccasins, new blue broadcloth shawls, plaited hair and clean faces looked almost good enough to kiss." He attended a dance in an Indian lodge, which was lighted with birchbark tapers. When he and a companion attempted to join the girls, they stopped their

Bronze bust of Chief Buffalo made in 1858 as a copy of an 1855 marble bust, carved from life. Both stand in the U. S. Capitol.

A ferrotype of Michael De Perry and an unidentified child. De Perry witnessed the signing of the 1854 treaty at La Pointe and migrated to Red Cliff with Buffalo's band.

The Indian Cemetery on Madeline Island near the modern marina, photographed around the turn of the century.

Nebraska Row before its plantings transformed the original pasture. Treaty Hall appears at the left.

The Protestant mission house built in 1834. Later it became a resort, and now a portion of the building houses the village post office near the La Pointe dock.

The Haecker cottage, one of the first on Nebraska Row, with some members of the Woods family posed before it.

Front porch of Coolepark Manor, now the Chateau Madeleine, originally the vacation home of the Albert Gregory Hull family.

A party of summer residents in the bow of the **Gee Whiz,** *probably going to or from Bayfield. Some visitors favored needlework, as demonstrated by the woman wearing the pince nez.*

A picnic on Basswood Island in 1916. Mrs. James Logan Abernathy, of Leavenworth, Kansas, and Kansas City, Missouri, dominates the scene.

WHi(X3)27832

The Omaha Railway's Island View Hotel in Bayfield, which catered to tourists for only seventeen years, 1883 to 1900, and was razed in 1913.

WHi(X3)27578

Frederick Prentice's Cedar Bark Lodge on Hermit Island. One of the most elegant retreats of the 1890's, it sported four fireplaces, some plumbing, and an observation tower.

The **Lizzie W.** in a fair blow getting away from the Old Mission resort dock. The **Perhaps** rests at anchor behind the **Lizzie,** and the village of La Pointe appears in the far right background.

Boats and the shoreline frame Soldier's Rock, just east of Madeline Island, in the late 1890's. Only a trace of the rock remains.

The Protestant Church, erected in 1839 by Sherman Hall, on its original site southeast of the La Pointe dock. It was moved in 1901 and collapsed in 1943.

The Roman Catholic church of 1841, decorated for a special occasion. The church burned in 1901 and was replaced by the existing structure.

A lumber camp at Big Bay on Madeline Island, an area now devoted to a state park.

The Washburn Stone Company quarry near Houghton Point. The Fred Pillsbury mansion in Minneapolis was one of many private and public structures built of Washburn Company sandstone.

The village of Bayfield as it appeared about 1888. Fish company warehouses dot the waterfront. The Island View Hotel is to the right of center.

The old Bayfield County Courthouse in Bayfield, built of locally quarried brownstone. The county seat was transferred to Washburn in 1892.

The Madeline Island Historical Museum, dedicated in June, 1958, and given to the State Historical Society of Wisconsin by Mr. and Mrs. Leo Capser in 1969.

dancing, and the two men entertained the mirthful assembly with a waltz.

PROSPECTS for the fur company's fishing enterprises looked bright in 1835. Company employees and Indians had fished for their own small commercial enterprises from at least 1830 on. Lake Superior also provided five abundant varieties of fish: whitefish, trout, herring, siscowet, and pickerel. These were relatively unknown in eastern markets, but it was believed that consumers would develop a taste for them, particularly consumers who lived in the Ohio River valley, which was remote from Atlantic fisheries.

The company proceeded cautiously at first and sought promising fishing banks. It tried Isle Royale, because it was known that the North West Company had fished the region successfully. Other excellent fishing waters were found off the Apostles, and minor fisheries were situated at other places on the south and northwestern shores of Lake Superior.

By late 1836, 1,000 barrels of salted fish were shipped from La Pointe, and twice that many in 1837. To Crooks' dismay, some of the 1837 barrels contained spoiled fish, caused by delays in salting them. Then the Panic of 1837 deflated prices disastrously from $12 to $10 a barrel. Crooks took matters into his own hands, personally inspected field operations in 1838, and thoroughly reorganized them. He ousted Warren in September, 1838, accusing him of inattention to duty and misadministration. He appointed Charles Borup as factor, in part because of gratitude for Borup's having refused an offer from a rival company in 1837. Borup, a Dane, operated the Northern Outfit very successfully for his Scottish master.

Crooks' native thrift often had an unpleasant side. One of the economies he instituted in 1839, at the close of the fishing season, was to send the fisheries' employees (coopers, foremen, and others) to La Pointe, where they could be housed and fed and put to work for the winter. In 1835, when he launched his fishing business, he discharged thirty boatmen, mostly older employees with large families who had to be fed under the company's contract with them. As fishermen, however, they would not receive a family food allotment. Further, Crooks induced their

43

wives to cook for the firm's employees and to pack the fish and furs without pay. Miscreant workers were sometimes beaten up and cudgeled on official order.

Such stringent measures worked. In 1838, the company packed 4,000 barrels of fish; in 1839, more than 5,000. The market turned incredibly sour, however, and the fish remained in the warehouses at Detroit. Company officers instructed their men to set the nets desultorily for the next two seasons so they could use up their supply of salt. In 1841, Crooks looked southward and unloaded 1,200 barrels there, and that summer he halted fishing operations entirely except for a few boats around Isle Royale, which caught rations for company employees.

Cessation of American Fur Company fishing operations did not halt all seining at La Pointe. In 1849, about 1,000 barrels were salted there, but comparable statistics are not available for much of the time since. In 1888 a Wisconsin state agency began keeping sketchy records of the pounds of fish caught in the Bayfield district, most of the catch coming from Apostle Islands waters. An amazing commercial growth, encouraged by the state, occurred between 1888 and 1896. In the first year, 1,766,665 pounds of fish valued at $45,281.52 were caught, and 147 employees were active in the industry; by 1896, 7,880,200 pounds were caught, and 160 persons were employed in the industry. Official reports ceased thereafter until 1940. In the three decades since then, fish production has varied considerably. The sea lamprey wiped out the lake trout population, but controls over the lamprey and efforts to reintroduce the trout from hatchery stock have succeeded, although the catch still is only a tenth of the usual 500,000 to 700,000-pound total annual figures of the 1940's. Whitefish production has fluctuated almost as wildly, and the smelt catch, which used to account for less than 500 pounds annually, now accounts for a half million pounds. La Pointe, however, no longer has a full-time fisherman. The last was hired by Wisconsin to operate its fishing research boat beginning in 1970. Some part-time fishermen still berth their boats on Madeline Island, but the giant fish warehouses of the Booth Fisheries at Bayfield stand empty, replaced by modern refrigeration and freezing techniques.

Problems with fishing were only part of the load thrust on Crooks' shoulders in the early 1840's. His Western Outfit was tottering in its competition with the Chouteau enterprises. Parts of the Northern Department had become unprofitable, owing to the influx of settlers. And finally, warm weather during the winter of 1841-1842 reduced the quality of the furs. Accordingly, in 1842 Crooks sold the Western Outfit, closed the Detroit Department, and reduced Northern Department operations to a minimum. He left only the Northern Outfit, based at La Pointe, relatively unaffected, although without its fishing operation. After 1842, the once continent-spanning fur empire confined its operations to Lake Superior. The retrenchment succeeded. A little more than a year after bankruptcy, the company paid its creditors a 25 per cent dividend. Under the continued watchfulness of Borup, the Northern Outfit produced more profit in 1842-1843 than in any other year. On December 31, 1847, the American Fur Company paid its debtors in full and ceased field operations, although it continued to exist as a corporation for some years. Dr. Borup moved to St. Paul, Minnesota, and became a successful financier. Lyman Warren died at La Pointe in 1847.

The American Fur Company's struggle for solvency at La Pointe was only one of several struggles taking place there in the 1830's and 1840's. Others included a Protestant-Catholic tug-of-war over the Chippewa, a Chippewa contretemps with the United States over mineral lands and reservations, and the economic community's attempts to establish non-fur enterprises there, all more or less interrelated.

As for the Protestant-Catholic struggle, before 1835 Sherman Hall had had the Indian mission field to himself. He had not erected a church, but he had built a mission house where he lived and conducted his school. His labors came to the attention of Father Frederic Baraga, an Austrian by birth who had been working on the Upper Lakes at Arbre Croche since 1831. By 1835 he was pleading for a transfer to La Pointe, whose Indians had requested a resident priest. Without receiving permission either from his bishop or from government agents who licensed missionaries, Baraga set out. The Roman Catholics among American Fur Company employees at La Pointe accommodated him, as the Protestants had the Reverend Mr. Hall. Within twelve days, Catholics at La Pointe erected a log church about 100 feet south of the Indian Cemetery near the modern marina. A growing congregation necessitated a new church in 1841 on the site of the present one. That church burned in 1901 and was replaced by the current structure.

Before Baraga arrived, Hall had concentrated on education and Christian instruction. He maintained high standards for converts, and their small number disappointed him. The school, too, bothered him. "There is much irregularity in the attendance of the pupils, owing to the mode of subsistence among the Indians, their migratory habits, instability of character, and the little interest they take in the education of their children, and in improvement generally," he complained. Baraga's arrival also annoyed him. The government policy was to grant an agency exclusive mission rights within a district, so American religious institutions would appear united and not confuse Indians by their diversity. He successfully kept Baraga from receiving federal funds to launch a school, and he also successfully petitioned for private funds to erect his own church—one of the first Protestant houses of worship in Wisconsin. He built it in 1839 in the new village, about 200 yards southeast of the fur company's dock, between the road and the beach. It, too, was a log structure covered with clapboards, with seats for 150 to 200 persons and a nicely finished, plaster-like interior. Hall's church was used by a variety of Protestant congregations during its lifetime, and in 1901 it was moved from the village to a site just south of the 1835 mission house. It stood there until 1943, when it collapsed. Its interior walls had by then been covered with squares of birchbark, and it looked far more rustic than the "finished" church which Hall described in 1839.

The Protestant mission further responded to Baraga's efforts by adding five persons to its staff, notably the Reverend Leonard H. Wheeler. Wheeler and his family soon became fixtures in the area. Both Hall and Wheeler believed that the Indian merely required education in order to be assimilated into white society, not recognizing the validity of his Indian religion, ethics, culture, tradition, and skills. Accordingly, Hall taught his charges traditional subjects, both in English and in Chippewa, but emphasizing English except in courses on Christianity, for which he used a Chippewa New Testament. Baraga, in turn, complained that Hall's better bilingual students received too much attention from U.S. officials, and the priest pleaded for permission to establish a school that would emphasize Chippewa language

46

instruction. Hall was not without sympathy for Indians, however. Every March he suspended school for a time so his pupils could participate in the annual maple-sugar-making exodus. He supported health care for Indians, and after eighteen died in a smallpox epidemic in 1847 he instructed an aide to vaccinate as many Chippewa as possible at the annuity payments on Madeline Island. He also encouraged agricultural education and the presence of a government-paid blacksmith who lived among the Chippewa.

Indian agricultural education was the specialty of the Reverend Mr. Wheeler. He found no suitable farmland on Madeline Island, and in 1845 he selected a site at what is now Odanah, Wisconsin, on the Bad River Reservation, east of Ashland. Chippewa had tilled the land there previously, they hunted and fished near it, they gathered their wild rice from the adjoining Kakagon Sloughs, and they tapped its sugar bush. Some Protestant Chippewa moved there, along with the Wheelers and their staff. Six years later, Wheeler reported happily that the Indians' crops had enabled them to survive several winters without going further into debt with the traders, who previously had profited because of Chippewa reliance upon a single crop—maple sugar.

Hall and Baraga both loathed introduction of liquor among the Chippewa, which was a curse to the tribe and its white neighbors. Some of their colleagues blamed the Indian ("his apathy, brutality, fondness for activity without labor, ingrain perfidy, shameless mendicancy, mere animal existence"); some blamed traders ("unprincipled wretches, rascals, robbers") in this dilemma. Critics of the whisky sellers said they concocted their product from a little whisky, some tobacco, and a lot of water. The traders then apportioned the contents of their barrels, kegs, and demijohns into pint bottles, which they sold at top dollar. Because the liquor trade with Indians was illegal, ruses were devised: liquor was shipped as dry goods, even as corn. U.S. Indian subagents at La Pointe destroyed what they found, but they found only a fraction of the available supply. Justice evaded Indians in this situation. Chippewa complained "that when Indians are guilty of outrages upon whites they are *punished*, while like acts are committed by whites upon Indians, and they *go free*." Official policy supported the Indian, but lack of personnel and remoteness rendered the policy unenforceable.

WHILE Hall and Baraga competed for the souls of the Chippewa, the federal government negotiated for their lands and mineral wealth. The Indians at La Pointe had come to the attention of the U.S. government in 1826 when U.S. Indian Commissioner Thomas L. McKenney visited there in July. (It was he who called the island "a fairy scene.") McKenney said the island should have a subagency for regulation of the Chippewa, but his recommendation was not realized for a decade. It finally was adopted in the wake of an 1837 treaty with the Chippewa, in which the tribe's bands from the Upper Mississippi and Chippewa rivers regions sold the United States a huge tract in northwestern Wisconsin and eastern Minnesota. Northern Michigan and the land directly south of Lake Superior, which were owned by the Lake Superior bands, were excluded. The government established its subagency at La Pointe and summoned the bands there for payments. The Lake Superior bands grew jealous when they saw others receiving government money, and in 1840 the La Pointe subagent reported they "are desirous of selling." He also noted that a treaty with the Lake Superior bands might weaken the appeal of British representatives, who exercised influence "by means of gratuities," accompanied by "pompous speeches," all of which were delivered to the Chippewa on a Canadian island in Lake Huron. Indians from La Pointe continued to travel there, and to the Red River, to receive gifts from the British as late as 1845.

These complications among the Chippewa and federal covetousness for their copper lands developed simultaneously. Douglass Houghton in 1840 and 1844 reawakened interest in Upper Michigan's copper country by extolling its potential in petitions to secure funds for geological expeditions. A youthful colleague of his, Charles Whittlesey, no doubt informed his father, a former congressman from Ohio, about the rich mineral deposits on the south shore of Lake Superior, and several Ohioans soon appeared among the developers in the region. Young Whittlesey maintained an interest in prospecting, and in 1848 discovered the Gogebic iron range in Michigan and Wisconsin, a companion to the earlier-discovered Marquette and Penokee ranges. Within six years, Charles' brother Asaph appeared in Chequamegon and founded the community of Ashland.

The result of these various coincidences was another treaty drawn at La Pointe in 1842 between the Lake Superior Chippewa and the U.S. government. One clause permitted the President to remove any Indian from mineral lands, which, to the confusion of the Chippewa chiefs who signed the document, was soon interpreted by the government to mean the whole of northern Wisconsin and Michigan. Mining developments predictably did occur in the ceded territory, and on February 6, 1850, President Zachary Taylor implemented the clause and ordered the Chippewa to move west to Sandy Lake and later to the Crow Wing River, both in Minnesota. A few Indians complied and moved from Chequamegon in May, 1850, motivated in part by the closing of the La Pointe subagency and its removal to Minnesota. Most of the Lake Superior Chippewa, however, remained, and Missionary Hall tarried with them. Finally he capitulated in 1853 and also moved to Minnesota, where he established a manual training school and supported agricultural and blacksmithing programs. A few months later he resigned and lived out his life in Minnesota as a minister and public educator.

Chippewa recalcitrance, supported by Hall, proved successful shortly after he moved. In 1854 the government negotiated another treaty at La Pointe, using as its headquarters the home of a former American Fur Company official. The house, near the north edge of the present village, was thereafter called Treaty Hall; it passed from hand to hand, later being transformed into an inn and ultimately burning in 1923. The treaty divided the La Pointe Chippewa into two bands, the Red Cliff and the Bad River—the Roman Catholic group agreeing to settle along the cliffs at the tip of Bayfield Peninsula; the Protestant group agreeing to accept the Bad River grounds and the historic Chequamegon Point and 200 acres on the northern edge of Madeline Island for fishing operations. The first Indian signature on the treaty was that of Chief Buffalo of the La Pointe band, who, with Hole-in-the-Day from Minnesota, is credited with retaining for the Chippewa some of their historic territory. In February, 1855, Chief Buffalo traveled to Washington to assist in negotiations for a further treaty between the U.S. and some Minnesota Chippewa, and while he was there his bust was modeled for decorating the U.S. Capitol, which was then being enlarged. Buffalo died later in 1855, having seen the successful

49

start of improvements on the Red Cliff lands. He was buried in the Indian Cemetery on Madeline Island, and his vandalized gravestone can be seen there yet.

Protestant efforts among the Indians at La Pointe ceased in 1853, and the government's financial support for education was contracted to Bishop Baraga. Wheeler continued the mission at Bad River until 1866, when he retired to Beloit, Wisconsin, and began a windmill factory. The Presbyterian Church took over his mission and ran it until 1884, then abandoned the field. Again the Catholic Church assumed charge, and it continues a school at Odanah.

Emphasis upon mineral resources near the Apostles had an impact far more spectacular than confinement of the Chippewa to reservations. The rich copper mines demanded improved transportation facilities to ship the metal to the east. The magnificent forests, too, lured developers who also required transportation. Railroad construction was proceeding slowly and expensively towards the north—too slowly for entrepreneurs—so the logical route was by way of Lake Superior and Lake Huron, which only required a canal and locks at Sault Ste. Marie to make them financially advantageous. The canal opened in 1855, and even before it was finished it brought a flood of investors to Chequamegon.

La Pointe benefited initially from the increased attention. In 1845, when Bayfield County was created, the village was made the county seat. (The county itself was called La Pointe until 1866.) In 1860, when Ashland County was created, the Apostles were attached to it, and from 1860 to 1863 the county seat was shifted to Ashland. It lost its status to La Pointe from 1863 to 1871, owing to population loss because of the Panic of 1857 and the Civil War, but regained it and has served as the administrative center for the region ever since. La Pointe also acquired a small lumber mill. Its water-powered saws in 1850 turned out 70,000 feet of lumber, and they were the forerunners of several lumber operations on the island. Agriculture barely existed there in 1850. The only farm of notice was operated by Sherman Hall, and it amounted to only thirty acres.

In 1854, just before completion of the canal, Asaph Whittlesey and his family appeared at La Pointe on their way to the site of Ashland, with hopes of founding a town and advancing the

50

Whittlesey fortunes. A year later, Elisha Pike and his family were induced by a La Pointe entrepreneur to settle on the mainland near Bayfield and to operate a sawmill. The entrepreneur was Julius Austrian, who had been associated with the American Fur Company and the government land agency, and who became the island's chief promoter after the fur company pulled out. Then, in 1856, Henry M. Rice, a powerful businessman and politician of St. Paul, Minnesota, platted the community of Bayfield and interested his friends and associates in buying timber lands and in developing the area. The community was named for Rice's friend, Lieutenant Henry W. Bayfield, who had charted Lake Superior for the British. These men commanded large amounts of capital, and they were able to act on a grander scale than men like Julius Austrian, who had to pin his hopes to Madeline Island. By 1860 Austrian owned 4,000 acres of Madeline and had 150 acres under cultivation. He operated a cooperage which annually turned out 600 barrels for fish, and he owned the island's inn. Obviously Austrian hoped to wrench a fortune from the island and its environs.

Austrian's attempts at eminence attracted competitors. Chief among them was Benjamin Armstrong, an Alabama native who was married to an Indian woman and who immersed himself in Chippewa and northern Wisconsin lore. He owned about 1,100 acres on the island, of which 130 were cultivated. A second cooperage, too, existed on the island, but it made half barrels for fish. A fishing boat maker on Madeline crafted twenty-five boats in 1860, and a steam-powered sawmill turned out a million feet of lumber, presumably from island trees. Austrian left the island sometime before 1870 and followed earlier Chequamegon developers to St. Paul, where he became a commission merchant and transportation executive. He held some Madeline Island property until his death on March 18, 1891. His heirs sold bits of his land to persons interested in tourism and in building private summer homes.

The entrepreneur who seems to have taken the reins of development from Austrian was no stranger to the region. He was, in fact, a rival promoter to Whittlesey of Ashland in 1854, and a man who had visited the forests of the region years before for the American Fur Company, carrying a payroll to the headwaters of the St. Croix River. His name was Frederick

Prentice, reputedly the first white child born in Toledo, Ohio (in 1822), and a speculator on a far grander scale than Austrian, belonging in the league of Rice and the elder Whittlesey. By 1857 he had acquired land near Ashland and also among the Apostles, especially on Wilson or Hermit's Island. He claimed to have noticed at that time a similarity between the brownstone of the Apostles and an inferior, shelly product from Connecticut quarries, which already was used to face New York City brownstones. The Panic of 1857 ruined Prentice, and he returned to Toledo to recoup his fortunes.

Later a second claimant for developing quarries in Chequamegon appeared. He was Alanson Sweet, a Wisconsin land speculator and politician from territorial days, who allegedly headed a party of prospectors that spent fifteen months in 1867 and 1868 looking for a good quarry site in the region. Credit is given both Sweet and Prentice for opening the first quarry in 1868 on the southern end of Basswood Island. Stone drawn from it was used to build Milwaukee's courthouse (now replaced) in 1870. Competitive complications hurt the quarry industry during much of the period before 1900, and a severe depression in 1893, price cutting, over-capitalization, and a change in architectural fashion from dark to light stone doomed it.

Despite these problems, other quarries soon followed the Basswood operation. They included one on Stockton Island (1889) and Prentice quarries on Wilson Island (1891) and Houghton Point (1888). The latter was the region's largest, and it furnished stone for construction in ten states and forty cities, including New York and Chicago, where the famous Potter Palmer lived within walls made of Chequamegon sandstone. Also from Prentice's largest quarry was taken an obelisk for the Columbian Exposition in Chicago in 1893, an obelisk larger than Cleopatra's Needle in New York's Central Park. Prentice gave the giant stone to exposition officials with the proviso that they transport it. The task proved prohibitively expensive, and the stone was cut up and used elsewhere. Altogether at least ten quarries operated on the islands and along Bayfield Peninsula, both on its eastern and western shores. By 1910 the quarries were virtually defunct.

About the sandstone itself a geological controversy has fluttered quietly in academic circles since geologist Houghton's day.

Estimates of its age in geological time have ranged from as old as Precambrian to as young as Silurian, which is rather like insisting that a ship is either a submarine or an aircraft carrier. The most recent scholarship indicates that the sandstone was deposited during the latest part of the Precambrian period or the Cambrian period, which, to continue the nautical analogy, makes the Chequamegon stone a pontoon—half in water, half out—and dates it at about 600 million years old. Very much older rocks, however, exist in northern Wisconsin and northern Minnesota.

His quarry failures did not overly distress Prentice. He had made millions in silver and copper mining in Nevada and he had invested in oil in Pennsylvania. He may well have regarded his northern Wisconsin holdings as a sentimental bagatelle. In 1895 he erected a large shingle-style lodge on Wilson's Island, supposedly for a bride (Prentice was then seventy-three) who inspected the place and detested it instantly. It sported four fireplaces carved of Chequamegon sandstone and an exterior covered with cedar bark shakes, hence Cedar Bark Lodge. It was not occupied after 1898 and fell victim to vandals and neglect. Finally it was razed in the 1930's. Prentice's affection for Ashland manifested itself in the gift of a park for the city. Some evidence exists that he first tried to develop the park as a profitable spa, and that he was moved to generosity after the failure of his quarries. Prentice's home in old age was in New York, where from offices on Broadway he stretched financial tentacles as far as South America. He maintained a mansion in Toledo, Ohio, and another along the Hudson River north of New York. He died at the age of ninety-one in 1913.

IN contrast to quarrying, lumbering and mining and their related industries flourished in Chequamegon. Even Madeline Island benefited for a while. R. D. Pike established a shingle mill at La Pointe in 1866, just east of the village dock. On May 17, 1869, the boiler exploded, killed a workman, injured several others, and touched off a fire that destroyed many structures, including some relic American Fur Company buildings. Pike thereupon moved his mill to Bayfield, where it prospered. Elsewhere in Chequamegon, the lumbering situation improved with construction of the Wisconsin Central Railway in 1877 between Ashland and Milwaukee. The line boasted some of the most spectacular railroad mileage in the state, including the famous White River bridge that soared 107 feet over the stream below. The completed railroad link prompted construction of numerous sawmills along Ashland's waterfront. The community of Washburn was founded as a lumber town in 1879, and soon mills were built on the west side of the peninsula, at Cornucopia, Herbster, and Port Wing. According to some accounts, the seasonal influx of men from the pineries transformed somnolent Chequamegon into a veritable Sodom, but La Pointe and the Apostles escaped the reputations earned by their neighbors. The era of lumbering ended in the region in 1924 with the closing of the last mill.

Mining created hubbub in Chequamegon in the late nineteenth century, and for a time it certainly involved Bayfield, which still served as a port city for the peninsula, owing to Ashland's unimproved and treacherous harbor. Iron deposits in northern Wisconsin had been found long before the railroad arrived, but it took a boom to establish an ore industry. Credit for the boom usually is given to N. D. Moore for an 1872 discovery. In fact, however, the rich Gogebic range was located by Charles Whittlesey in 1848. Transportation shortcomings delayed development until 1884, when the first ore was taken from the Gogebic and shipped by rail to Marquette, Michigan. In 1885 the Milwaukee, Lake Shore & Western Railroad (a part of the modern North Western Road) reached Ashland from Ironwood, Michigan, and in 1886 the first ore dock was built at Ashland. (Ore demanded water transportation, and had to be hauled by rail from the mines to the ships.) Phenomenal growth accompanied the arrival of the ore-shipping industry to Ashland. In 1880, the entire county had a population of 353 persons; in 1890, the city alone had 9,956 persons. The population boom encouraged real estate speculation in the community and on mineral lands. From 1886 to 1888 prospectors and promoters poured into the town; barrooms and iniquitous dens flourished, and ordinary householders charged premium rates for sleeping quarters. Ultimately the paper fortunes vanished, and most of their owners with them.

Mining on the Gogebic went along smoothly until the Depression, when some mines closed temporarily. They reopened and continued operating until the 1960's, when they were closed one by one. The last, the Cary mine owned by Pickands Mather & Co., ceased functioning on January 28, 1965, a victim of competition from low-grade taconite pellets and high-grade ores from other sources. It had been in operation from 1886 and had produced more than eighteen million tons of ore.

Tiny Bayfield profited from the iron industry. Henry M. Rice, the St. Paul businessman, U.S. Senator, and railroad scion, used his influence to have the Omaha line terminate, not at the logical port of Ashland, but at Bayfield, the logical jumping-off point for Rice to visit his holdings on the peninsula and Rocky Island. Great tootings and shouts heralded the arrival of the first train to Bayfield on October 12, 1883.

Bayfield harbor's natural advantages over Ashland's were not lost on William F. Dalrymple, the next entrepreneur to attempt development of Bayfield. Dalrymple was a Pennsylvanian who, with his brother Oliver, owned and managed their own and others' vast wheatlands in North Dakota. The brothers operated their business and the wheat businesses of railroad magnates from offices in St. Paul and Pennsylvania, and their connections with Northern Pacific Railroad officials doubtless led to William's investments in the Bayfield area. The brothers disagreed about the best means to market the wheat—through the Red River Valley or via the Great Lakes. To advance his Great Lakes scheme, William in 1878 bought a Wisconsin railroad charter from a line that had never built a mile of track. He reorganized it, planned to extend it to St. Louis through Milwaukee and Peoria, conducted engineering surveys, and negotiated with other lines. But his plans failed. He completed only sixteen miles of track by 1898, and it carried a negligible amount of local and passenger traffic. The leased shipment of lumber and logs proved far more profitable to Dalrymple, who died in 1901.

The success of the mining and lumbering industries attracted the Du Pont Company's attention about 1902. Both required large amounts of blasting materials, as did the waning quarry industry and the farmers who were clearing fields from the cutover forests. Du Pont arranged for purchase of a giant tract of land south of Washburn upon which to build an explosives factory, and operations began there in 1905. The resulting community, called Barksdale after a Du Pont executive, drew workers from Washburn and Ashland. In 1912, TNT production began there, and at the outbreak of World War II Barksdale had the only TNT factory in the U.S. Hundreds of workers were trained at Barksdale during the war for employment in TNT manufacturing plants that were hastily constructed elsewhere. Production ceased there in 1971, but the company still owns the large plant site.

DURING the heyday of lumbering and mining, Bayfield and Madeline Island began to feel the impact of the modern industry of tourism. The communities themselves did little to promote it. Promotion had been given them by early visitors, railroads, and devotees of the region, many of whom had business interests nearby. Among early famous visitors were Mrs. Abraham Lincoln and perhaps her son Thomas (Tad) Lincoln, who stepped ashore long enough at La Pointe in 1868 to visit Bishop Baraga's church, but who probably did not tarry at the inn, of which it was said, "it's full of knot holes and the men snore something awful." President Calvin Coolidge and his family also paid a visit to La Pointe exactly sixty years later. In 1877 the Wisconsin Central Railroad opened the Hotel Chequamegon in Ashland, and it lured tourists to the region. The hotel closed in 1913. The Omaha line followed suit with a tourist hotel at Bayfield, the Island View Hotel. It was a multiple-porticoed structure with a grand ballroom, parqueted floors, magnificent views, and a short life. It was built in 1883, closed in 1900, and razed in 1913.

Occasional attempts to launch resort developments on Madeline Island were made in the late nineteenth and early twentieth centuries, but they had only modest success. In 1887, a Milwaukee-based resort company led by George Francis Thomas vainly attempted to sell shares and to erect a resort community. Thomas later sold plots to many cottagers and for a short time he ran an inn at Treaty Hall, where board and room cost $8 to $10 a week. Again in the early 1900's, the Soo Line promoted construction of a large inn, golf course, and numerous small cottages, also to no avail. Relatively small resorts have succeeded on the island, but in the main the summer residents proceeded on their own to build the homes and cottages that dot Madeline and a few of the smaller Apostles.

56

Modern summer residences on Madeline Island date to 1894, when the Reverend Thomas Gordon Grassie and his family of Ashland settled in two small shacks and made plans for building a bona fide cottage. Grassie was associated with what is now Northland College at Ashland, and when the time came to begin construction in 1895, he was surprised to learn that John O'Brien of St. Paul already had erected a cottage along the southwest shore of the island, just east of the municipal dock. O'Brien's father was Dillon O'Brien, a lay teacher in Bishop Baraga's parochial school at La Pointe beginning in 1857 and later a St. Paul resident. Soon a string of cottages appeared near John O'Brien's, many of them built and occupied by other members of his family, as they are by the present generations of his descendants. Locally the string of summer dwellings is called O'Brien's Row.

A second and more famous row of houses—Nebraska Row—graces the shore north of the village dock. Like the O'Brien cottages they are occupied mainly by descendants and family connections of the founder of the row, Colonel Frederick M. Woods of Lincoln, Nebraska. Woods spent some time in Bayfield and, in 1898, on Madeline at a small cottage next to the Old Mission, which had been renovated as a hotel from the Protestant mission. Woods desired a bowling alley next to his cottage, and the Old Mission resort owner, who catered to a clerical crowd, refused to allow it. The upshot was that the colonel built his own establishment on Nebraska Row, then a treeless pasture. Woods publicized the island's charms among his friends and induced many to build homes, including Hunter L. Gary, a Missouri telephone entrepreneur and founder of General Telephone. The two men together entertained President Coolidge during his 1928 visit. Woods' personality and magnetism have been credited with establishing the island's special ambience of active leisure and a steadfast and selective summer population. It was not long before cottages sprang up along the rim of the island, especially the southern half.

The result of the kind of selectivity exercised by Woods and his friends has been a rather homogeneous Madeline Island summer population. Despite the provenance of the various vaca- tioners — Beloit, Milwaukee, St. Paul, Ashland, Lincoln — they all came to know one another and the permanent residents as well, although they vastly exceeded the year-around population in number. It is estimated that 2,000 or 3,000 persons spend about three months annually on Madeline, but no more than 150 to 250 live there twelve months a year. The island in effect became a transient small town, and the permanent residents and long-time cottagers regarded one another affectionately and with a relative lack of the suspicion that usually characterizes resort communities. The two sets of residents mingled comfortably at summer clam bakes, where fish and other delectables were steamed over seaweed-covered coals. As time passed, permanent residents began to rely upon summer visitors for employment, and they depended less and less upon fishing and agriculture. The summer traffic brought improved communications and utilities as well–advantages which redounded to everyone.

As generation of summer residents succeeded generation, some became interested in preserving Madeline's past. Two especially emerged as historian and museologist, Hamilton Nelson Ross and Leo Capser, both familiar with La Pointe from childhood and both successful businessmen. In 1960, Ross, from the Chicago area, published a thorough history of La Pointe. Beginning in 1955, Capser and his wife Bella, from St. Paul, developed the Madeline Island Historical Museum. It was constructed from a surviving American Fur Company building, Gus Dahlin's barn, the old La Pointe jail, and the Old Sailor's Home, built as a memorial to a drowned seaman. The amateur archeologist, Al Galazen, contributed his artifacts and bossed the construction. The Capsers financed the venture whenever they could not scrounge materials. Residents contributed 90 per cent of the museum's artifacts from all periods of the island's life, again testifying to the amalgamation of the island's two communities. The museum opened June 15, 1958. On April 11, 1969, the Capsers transferred ownership and operation to the State Historical Society of Wisconsin, which runs it as part of an extensive historic sites program.

Public development of Madeline Island began in 1963, when Wisconsin's Conservation Commission established Big Bay State Park on the eastern shore. The state gradually expanded the park, and plans include an area totaling 2,707 acres. Camping and boating facilities are available seasonally.

Federal interest in the Apostles area was initiated by Senator Gaylord Nelson of Wisconsin in the early 1960's, and on June 27, 1969, Congress established the Apostle Islands National Lakeshore Area. The area will include twenty of the twenty-two islands (Madeline and Long islands being excluded) and a ten-mile-long strip of land along Bayfield Peninsula's western shore, stretching from Cornucopia to the Red Cliff reservation. The stretch includes the famous, colorful pillared rocks, which have fascinated visitors for 300 years. Campsites are planned for Sand Island, Rocky Island, and Stockton Island. The aim is to maintain the islands and the lakeshore in a wilderness state and to encourage preservation.

Madeline Island has been omitted from the wilderness area, and in consequence has undergone major changes at the hands of developers. The developments have been spearheaded by Theodore S. Gary, son of the man who entertained President Coolidge and a principal stockholder and officer in his family's corporations. Gary also heads the companies which built the golf course and marina on the island, and heads another which is to build hundreds of luxury vacation homes there. The alterations have been dramatic. Where French traders once had forts and Indian Villages once stood, vacationers now play golf. A quiet lagoon, where the dip of a canoe paddle once constituted an interruption, now shelters gasoline-powered pleasure craft.

What would early entrepreneurs like Crooks, Prentice, Austrian, and Dalrymple have thought of it? They loved Chequamegon and Madeline Island, and they respected the region's possibilities. Chequamegon responded by yielding some profit, but its facade was not changed significantly because of their efforts. Even the trees that had been removed by lumbermen grew back, restoring the fairyland appearance of the 1820's. Will Chequamegon continue to resist and restore itself, or will tourism finally conquer the wilderness that enticed so many generations of investors?

THE AUTHOR

JOHN O. HOLZHUETER, associate editor of the *Wisconsin Magazine of History,* has been a member of the Society's research and editorial staff since 1973 and is well known throughout the state for his weekly broadcasts about Wisconsin history prepared for Wisconsin Public Radio. Besides speaking and writing on Wisconsin topics, he has acted as a bibliographic and reference consultant for academic and lay historians from around the country and has been closely involved with the six-volume *History of Wisconsin* project for nearly two decades.